FROM FAIRY TALES TO REAL LIFE

STORIES OF LOVE AT FIRST SIGHT THAT WILL MAKE YOU BELIEVE

ASHWINI.R

Made with ❤ on the Notion Press Platform
www.notionpress.com

I Hope you believe in love, because i belive in you

Contents

Foreword

Fairy tales and romance novels have long fueled our fascination with love at first sight. But is it just a myth or can it actually happen in real life? Many believe that love of which side you're on, theres no denying that some stories are so captivating that they make you want to believe. In this article, we'll explore some of the most remarkable tales of love at first sight that will make you question the notion that its just a figment of our imagination. From chance encounters to destiny, these stories will take you on a journey of love and all ways it can manifest. So sit back, relax, and prepare to be inspired by these stories that will reignite your belief in the power of love at first sight.

Preface

THE SCIENCE BEHIND LOVE AT FIRST SIGHT~~~

Although love at first sight is often dismissed as a romantic fantasy, there is scientific evidence to support its existence. According to researchers, the experience of love at first sight is triggered by a complex interplay of hormones and neurotransmitters that flood the brain when we encounter someone we find attractive. These chemical reactions can cause feelings of euphoria, excitement, and a sence of connection with the other person.

Studies have also shown that love at first sight can be influenced by external factors such as physical appearence,body language, and even the environment. For example, being in a romantic setting or experiencing a thrilling activity together can heighten the intensity of the emotions.

Acknowledgements

Ĩ would like to thank my parents for their marvelous support~

Prologue

FAMOUS LOVE AT FIRST SIGHT STORIES:

~~~From litrature to Hollywood, love at first sight has been a popular theme in storytelling throughout history. Some of the most famous examples include:
~~~

1

ROMEO AND JULIET

The tragic love story of Romeo and Juliet is perhaps the most iconic tale of love at first sight.

Romeo the son of montague, runs into his cousin Benvolio, who had earlier seen Romeo moping in a grove of sycamores.Aftersome prodding by Benvolio, Romeo confides that he is in love with Rosaline, a woman who does not return his affections. Benvolio counsels him to forget this woman and find another, more beautiful one, but Romeo remains despondent.

Meanwhil, Paris a kingsman of the Prince, seeks Juliet

hand in marriage. Her father Capulet, though happy at the match, asks Paris to wait two years, since Juliet is not yet even fourteen. Capulet dispatches a servant with a list of people to invite to a masquerade and feast he traditionally holds. He invites Paris to the feast, hoping that Paris will begin to win Juliet's heart.

Romeo and Benvolio, still discussing Rosaline, encounter the Capulet servant bearing the list of invitations. Benvolio suggests that they attend, since that will allow Romeo to compare his beloved to other beautiful women of Verona. Romeo agrees to go with Benvolio to the feast, but only because Rosaline, whose name he reads on the list, will be there.

In Capulet's household, young Juliet talks with her mother, Lady Capulet, and her nurse about the possibility of marrying Paris. Juliet has not yet considered marriage, but agrees to look at Paris during the feast to see if she thinks she could fall in love with him.

The feast begins. A melancholy Romeo follows Benvolio and their witty friend Mercutio to Capulet's house. Once inside, Romeo sees Juliet from a distance and instantly falls in love with her; he forgets about Rosaline completely. As Romeo watches Juliet, entranced, a young Capulet, Tybalt, recognizes him, and is enraged that a Montague would sneak into a Capulet feast. He prepares to attack, but Capulet holds him back. Soon, Romeo speaks to Juliet, and the two experience a profound attraction. They kiss, not even knowing each other's names. When he finds out from Juliet's nurse that she is the daughter of Capulet—his family's enemy—he becomes distraught. When Juliet learns that the young man she has just kissed is the son of Montague, she grows equally upset.

As Mercutio and Benvolio leave the Capulet estate, Romeo leaps over the orchard wall into the garden, unable to leave Juliet behind. From his hiding place, he sees Juliet in a window above the orchard and hears her speak his name. He calls out to her, and they exchange vows of love.

Romeo hurries to see his friend and confessor Friar Lawrence, who, though shocked at the sudden turn of Romeo's heart, agrees to marry the young lovers in secret since he sees in their love the possibility of ending the age-old feud between Capulet and Montague. The following day,

Romeo and Juliet meet at Friar Lawrence's cell and are married. The Nurse, who is privy to the secret, procures a ladder, which Romeo will use to climb into Juliet's window for their wedding night.

The next day, Benvolio and Mercutio encounter Tybalt—Juliet's cousin—who, still enraged that Romeo attended Capulet's feast, has challenged Romeo to a duel. Romeo appears. Now Tybalt's kinsman by marriage, Romeo begs the Capulet to hold off the duel until he understands why Romeo does not want to fight. Disgusted with this plea for peace, Mercutio says that he will fight Tybalt himself. The two begin to duel. Romeo tries to stop them by leaping between the combatants. Tybalt stabs Mercutio under Romeo's arm, and Mercutio dies. Romeo, in a rage, kills Tybalt. Romeo flees from the scene. Soon after, the Prince declares him forever banished from Verona for his crime. Friar Lawrence arranges for Romeo to spend his wedding night with Juliet before he has to leave for Mantua the following morning.

In her room, Juliet awaits the arrival of her new husband. The Nurse enters, and, after some confusion, tells Juliet that Romeo has killed Tybalt. Distraught, Juliet suddenly finds herself married to a man who has killed her kinsman. But she resettles herself, and realizes that her duty belongs with her love: to Romeo.

Romeo sneaks into Juliet's room that night, and at last they consummate their marriage and their love. Morning comes, and the lovers bid farewell, unsure when they will see each other again. Juliet learns that her father, affected by the recent events, now intends for her to marry Paris in just three days. Unsure of how to proceed—unable to reveal to her parents that she is married to Romeo, but unwilling to marry Paris now that she is Romeo's wife—Juliet asks her nurse for advice. She counsels Juliet to proceed as if Romeo were dead and to marry Paris, who is a better match anyway. Disgusted with the Nurse's disloyalty, Juliet disregards her advice and hurries to Friar Lawrence. He concocts a plan to reunite Juliet with Romeo in Mantua. The night before her wedding to Paris, Juliet must drink a potion that will make her appear to be dead. After she is laid to rest in the family's crypt, the Friar and Romeo will secretly retrieve her, and she will be free to live with Romeo, away from their parents' feuding.

Juliet returns home to discover the wedding has been moved ahead one day, and she is to be married tomorrow. That night, Juliet drinks the potion, and the Nurse discovers her, apparently dead, the next morning. The Capulets grieve, and Juliet is entombed according to plan. But Friar Lawrence's message explaining the plan to Romeo never reaches Mantua. Its bearer, Friar John, gets confined to a quarantined house. Romeo hears only that Juliet is dead.

Romeo learns only of Juliet's death and decides to kill himself rather than live without her. He buys a vial of poison from a reluctant Apothecary, then speeds back to Verona to take his own life at Juliet's tomb. Outside the Capulet crypt, Romeo comes upon Paris, who is scattering flowers on Juliet's grave. They fight, and Romeo kills Paris. He enters the tomb, sees Juliet's inanimate body, drinks the poison, and dies by her side. Just then, Friar Lawrence enters and realizes that Romeo has killed Paris and himself. At the same time, Juliet awakes. Friar Lawrence hears the coming of the watch. When Juliet refuses to leave with him, he flees alone. Juliet sees her beloved Romeo and realizes he has killed himself with poison. She kisses his poisoned lips, and when that does not kill her, buries his dagger in her chest, falling dead upon his body.

The watch arrives, followed closely by the Prince, the Capulets, and Montague. Montague declares that Lady Montague has died of grief over Romeo's exile. Seeing their children's bodies, Capulet and Montague agree to end their long-standing feud and to raise gold statues of their children side-by-side in a newly peaceful Verona.

2

Elizabeth Taylor and Richard Burton

The real-life romance between Elizabeth Taylor and Richard Burton is another classic example of love at first sight.

The first day that Elizabeth Taylor saw the handsome Welsh actor Richard Burton on the set of Cleopatra he walked over to her and whispered, "has anybody ever told you taht you're a very pretty girl?"

It was not a great pickup-line by anyone's standards, especially since Elizabeth, who was on the cusp of 30 and at the height of her smoldering sensuality, was already the most famous star of the twentieth century known for her raven hair and legendary blue eyes that some swore were an otherworldly shade of violet. “Here's the great lover,” she joked, “the great wit, the great intellectual of Wales, and he comes out with a line like that.” Plus, Richard's reputation as a married man with a penchant for seducing his leading ladies had preceded him.

But her feelings changed on January 22, 1962, when they filmed their first scene together. Elizabeth starred as

Cleopatra, the woman who had conquered empires, and Richard played Marc Antony, the powerful Roman general who became Cleopatra's lover. Richard, then thirty-six, had gone on a bender the night before, drinking everything he could get his hands on. It was five o'clock in the afternoon, and he had not slept for two nights. He got a cup of coffee, but he could not bring the cup to his lips because his hands were shaking so badly. He asked Elizabeth for help. "Hold this, love, will you hold it to my mouth?" She held the cup up to his mouth and started to giggle.

"He was such a slob," she said later, "he was such a mess, and I looked into those green eyes that were twinkling and smiling at me and he drank the whole mug and we kept staring at each other." She remembered, being so close to him, seeing the grog blossoms—the burst blood vessels on the face of a heavy drinker—and strangely falling for him in that moment. He was not the arrogant stage actor she had imagined, instead he was achingly vulnerable.

The feeling was mutual. "I fell in love at once," Richard said later. "She was like a mirage of beauty of the ages, irresistible like the pull of gravity."

The problem was that both of them were married, Elizabeth to singer Eddie Fisher and Richard to the actress Sybil Burton, with whom he shared two daughters. Fisher stopped coming to the set when Richard and Elizabeth had a scene together; their flirtation was too obvious and too humiliating. Sybil believed that her husband's affair with Elizabeth would be no different than all the others.

But there was no way to ignore them once they became a global phenomenon – Richard called it "Le Scan dale" - a love affair that marked the beginning of the world's obsession with celebrity. Long before "Brangelina," "Bennifer," and "Kimye," "Liz and Dick" practically invented the paparazzi. Images of them kissing on yachts in the Mediterranean and walking along Rome's fashionable Via Veneto knocked John Glenn's orbit of the Earth in 1962 off the front pages. "I've had affairs before," Richard told a publicist working on *Cleopatra*. "How did I know the woman was so fucking famous? She knocks Khrushchev off the front page."

Their affair was such enormous news that even the Vatican was paying attention. In an open letter in Vatican City's weekly newspaper, Elizabeth was charged with "erotic vagrancy" because she was sleeping with Burton while still married to Fisher (never mind that Richard was cheating on his wife too). The Vatican decried "this insult to the nobility of the hearth."

Elizabeth and Richard didn't let the moralizing stop them. Richard ended one note to Elizabeth with: "Would you, incidentally, permit me to fuck you this afternoon?" In another, he wrote: "I love you badly like a disease. I dream of you curled up asleep. I'm even jealous of the bed. . . ."

Eventually, they each got divorced and they were married in Montreal on March 15, 1964. Elizabeth was thirty-two and Richard was thirty-eight, he was her fifth husband and she became his second wife. The minister started the ceremony by saying, "You have gone through great travail in your love for each other." They had been hounded and harassed, pilloried and praised. They stayed up talking, laughing, and crying until 7:00 a.m. the next morning. "I'm so happy you can't believe it," Elizabeth gushed.

John Springer was Elizabeth's publicist during this period of her life and he had also represented Marilyn Monroe. "One thing Marilyn could do and Elizabeth can't do is walk on the street by herself," he said. "Marilyn could put on dark glasses or a dark wig or something, she could walk on the street." Elizabeth and Richard could not even leave their hotel room without being mobbed, which made them miserable.

Some time, Elizabeth dreamed, when they were older, they would put an end to their frenetic lifestyle. Richard would become a writer like he always wanted to and she would stop acting and take care of their home. She lit up at the mere idea of it; it gave her such pleasure to think of what it would be like to live a quiet life. In the end, it was a beautiful fantasy.

They found solace in each other. In 1969 Elizabeth wrote:

"As long as he loves her everything is O.K. pimples, stupid hips, double chins, and all—She loved him more than her life and always will.—Wife."

They starred in films together and made millions. But they possessed and craved each other one minute and could not bear the sight of each other the next. "We were like magnets," Elizabeth said, "alternately pulling toward each other and, inexorably, pushing away." For their 1966 masterpiece *Who's Afraid of Virginia Woolf?* Elizabeth won an Oscar for her incredible transformation as Martha and he did not. "Maybe I'm jealous of her power or something, I don't know," Richard once admitted.

It was a love too all-consuming to last. So many of Richard's letters to Elizabeth include apologies for whatever alcohol-fueled fight had taken place the night before. "I shall be good today and surprise you," he wrote on October 9, 1972. "Thank you for taking care of me yesterday."

After one particularly rough night Elizabeth wrote:

"Richard,

There have been times that I have loved you more than my life—and

more than my children.
Something must be very wrong with the two of us if I'm put in the position of having to take sides—having
to choose between
you or my kids.
Your behavior tonight has sickened me and I think made my children not like you very much—not
that you give a fuck. But they
do care about each other and I care about them.
Sorry about you."

"Liz and Dick" soon became the "Battling Burtons." We were "mutually self-destructive," Elizabeth said. "Maybe we have loved each other too much."

To mark their tenth wedding anniversary in 1974, Elizabeth wrote:

My darling (my still) my husband, I wish I could tell you of my love for you, of my fear, my delight, my pure animal pleasure of you—(with you)—my jealousy, my pride, my anger at you, at times. Most of all my love for you, and whatever love you can dole out to me—I wish I could write about it but I can't. I can only "boil and bubble" inside and hope you understand how I really feel.

Anyway I lust thee, your (still) wife. P.S. O'Love, let us never take each other for granted again! P.P.S. How about that—ten years!

A month later they announced that they would be getting a divorce. But they could not stay away from each other for long. On October 10, 1975, they married for the second time in a secret ceremony on the banks of a river in Botswana. She wrote in a diary entry: "We exchanged rings, fathomless looks, and were married once again, back where we belonged. Always belonged." Letters they wrote to each other after the ceremony reveal how much they wanted to start a new life together.

Elizabeth Taylor: The Grit & Glamour of an Icon

Dear Husb.,

How about that! You really are my husband again and I have news for you, there will be bloody no more marriages—or divorces.

We are stuck like chicken feathers to tar—for lovely always.

Do you realize that we shall grow old together and I know the best is yet to be!

Anyway, my little big one I love you and have a deep tranquility in my heart and the tug of love is over and we are one once more. I'm happy, I hope you are,

Yours Truly,

Wife

But on July 29, 1976, less than ten months after they married for a second time, Elizabeth and Richard were granted their second divorce. "I love Richard with every fiber of my soul," Elizabeth said, "but we can't be together." She was forty-four years old and alone, but she was determined to follow her own advice: "Pour yourself a drink," she famously advised the heartbroken, "put on some lipstick, and pull yourself together." She knew another love was waiting around the corner—and she was right.

3

Real-life stories of love at first sight

While love at first sight may be a popular theme in fiction, it also happens in real life. Here are some remarkable stories of people who fell in love at first sight:

~~~~~LETS FIND OUT!!
~~~~~

Chance encounters

Sometimes, love can strike when we least expect it. Take the case of 24-year-old Emily, who fell in love with a stranger on a train. She was on her way to work when she spotted a handsome man sitting across from her. They made eye contact and exchanged a smile, and Emily felt an instant connection. They struck up a conversation and ended up talking for the entire journey. When they arrived at their destination, the man asked for her phone number, and they've been together ever since.

Destiny

For some, love at first sight is a matter of destiny. This was the case for 27-year-old Alex, who fell in love with a woman he met while on vacation in Thailand. He was walking on the beach when he saw her sitting alone, looking out at the ocean. He felt drawn to her and went over to introduce himself. As they talked, they discovered that they had many things in common and felt an instant connection. Despite living on opposite sides of the world, they decided to give their relationship a chance and have been happily married for five years.

Serendipity

Sometimes, love at first sight can happen in the most unexpected places. This was the case for 32-year-old Sarah, who fell in love with a man she met while waiting in line at the grocery store. They struck up a conversation while waiting to pay, and Sarah felt an instant connection. As they talked, they discovered that they had many shared interests and values. They exchanged phone numbers and have been together ever since.

BTS nd ARMY

If you weren't already familiar with BTS, then let me introduce them to you

They are the global K-pop sensation likely came blazing onto your radar this past june.

I am sure BTS was a love at first sight for most of the ARMY's out there!

One of the reasons BTS has become so popular is their connection with their fans. BTS has gone to great lengths to create a personal relationship with their fans, often sharing personal stories and experiences through their music and social media.

BTS has also made a point to connect with their fans through their concerts and fan events. They take the time to interact with fans, often stopping to take selfies and share hugs. BTS's connection with their fans goes beyond just music; it is a personal relationship built on trust, respect, and mutual admiration.

BTS's connection with their fans has created a sense of loyalty and devotion that is rare in the music industry. Fans feel a deep sense of gratitude and affection towards BTS, and in return, BTS has shown their appreciation through their music and actions.

BTS is more than just a band; they are a cultural force that has captured the hearts of millions of fans around the world. Their music is not just catchy pop tunes, but a message of self-love, acceptance, and unity that resonates with people from all walks of life. BTS has created a community of fans who feel empowered and supported by their music, and who have found a sense of belonging in the BTS fandom.

BTS's success is a testament to the power of music to bring people together and create positive change in the world. Their impact on the music industry and pop culture is undeniable, and their legacy will continue to inspire and empower young people around the world for years to come. Whether you're a die-hard fan or just curious about the BTS phenomenon, there is no denying that BTS is more than just a band.

BORAHAE!

4

The psychology of love at first sight

While love at first sight may seem like a romantic fantasy, there's actually a lot of psychology behind it. According to psychologists, the experience of love at first sight is largely driven by our unconscious mind. When we encounter someone we find attractive, our brain automatically interprets the information and creates a mental image of the person. This image is then compared to our internal standards of attractiveness, and if there's a match, we experience a sense of attraction and connection.

In addition, love at first sight is also influenced by our past experiences and beliefs about love. People who have had positive experiences with love in the past are more likely to believe in love at first sight and to be open to the experience. Conversely, people who have had negative experiences may be more skeptical or guarded.

5

The debate around love at first sight

Despite the scientific evidence and real-life stories, the debate around love at first sight rages on. Some people argue that it's nothing more than a fleeting infatuation, while others believe that it's a genuine and powerful emotion.

One of the main criticisms of love at first sight is that it's based solely on physical attraction and doesn't take into account the person's character, values, or personality. Critics argue that a lasting relationship requires much more than just a momentary spark of attraction.

However, supporters of love at first sight point out that it's not just about physical attraction, but also about a sense of connection and compatibility that can be felt on a deeper level. They argue that love at first sight can be the start of a meaningful and lasting relationship.

6

The role of intuition in love at first sight

One of the unique aspects of love at first sight is the role of intuition. People who have experienced it often describe a strong sense of knowing that this person is "the one" or that they were meant to be together.

According to psychologists, intuition is an important part of the human mind that helps us make quick and accurate decisions based on limited information. When it comes to love at first sight, intuition may play a role in helping us recognize a potential partner who is compatible with us on a deeper level.

7

Can love at first sight lead to a lasting relationship?

The big question surrounding love at first sight is whether it can lead to a lasting relationship. While there's no guarantee that a relationship that starts with love at first sight will last, there are many examples of couples who have built long and happy lives together.

One of the keys to making love at first sight work is to approach the relationship with an open mind and heart. It's important to take the time to get to know the person and to build a strong foundation of trust and communication. It's also important to be realistic about the challenges that may arise and to work together to overcome them.

8

Tips for recognizing love at first sight and embracing it

If you're open to the idea of love at first sight, there are some things you can do to increase your chances of recognizing it when it happens:

-Be open to new experiences and opportunities to meet new people.

-Trust your instincts and be aware of the signs of attraction and connection.

-Don't dismiss a potential partner based solely on physical appearance.

-Take the time to get to know the person and build a strong foundation of trust and communication.

Once a wise woman told me" If we don't have trust, we don't have anything"

Love at first sight may be a controversial topic, but the stories and science behind it suggest that its a real and powerful emotion. Whether it's a chance encounter, destiny, or serendipity, there are many ways that love at first sight can manifest in our lives.

While there's no guarantee that a relationship that starts with love at first sight will last, it's worth embracing the possibilioty and approching it with an open mind and heart.Who knows - you just find your own fairytale ending.

Printed by Libri Plureos GmbH in Hamburg,
Germany